GREAT PRO SPORTS CHAMPIONSHIPS

GREAT NBA CHAMPIONSHIPS

by Ethan Olson

BrightPoint Press

San Diego, CA

© 2024 BrightPoint Press
an imprint of ReferencePoint Press, Inc.
Printed in the United States

For more information, contact:
BrightPoint Press
PO Box 27779
San Diego, CA 92198
www.BrightPointPress.com

ALL RIGHTS RESERVED.

No part of this work covered by the copyright hereon may be reproduced or used in any form or by any means—graphic, electronic, or mechanical, including photocopying, recording, taping, web distribution, or information storage retrieval systems—without the written permission of the publisher.

LIBRARY OF CONGRESS CATALOGING-IN-PUBLICATION DATA

Names: Olson, Ethan, author.
Title: Great NBA championships / By Ethan Olson.
Description: San Diego, CA : BrightPoint, [2024] | Series: Great pro sports championships | Includes bibliographical references and index. | Audience: Ages 13 | Audience: Grades 7–9
Identifiers: LCCN 2023015172 (print) | LCCN 2023015173 (eBook) | ISBN 9781678206567 (hardcover) | ISBN 9781678206574 (eBook)
Subjects: LCSH: National Basketball Association--Juvenile literature. | Basketball--Tournaments--United States--History--Juvenile literature. | Basketball players--United States--Juvenile literature.
Classification: LCC GV885.515.N37 .O47 2024 (print) | LCC GV885.515.N37 (eBook) | DDC 796.323/64--dc23/eng/20230404
LC record available at https://lccn.loc.gov/2023015172
LC eBook record available at https://lccn.loc.gov/2023015173

CONTENTS

AT A GLANCE	4
INTRODUCTION	6
WHERE LEGENDS ARE MADE	
CHAPTER ONE	10
CLASH OF THE TITANS	
CHAPTER TWO	22
ONE LAST SHOT	
CHAPTER THREE	34
THE BIG THREE	
CHAPTER FOUR	46
BRINGING IT HOME	
Glossary	58
Source Notes	59
For Further Research	60
Index	62
Image Credits	63
About the Author	64

AT A GLANCE

- The National Basketball Association (NBA) named its first champion in 1946–47, three years before the league took on its current name.

- Over their first seven meetings in the NBA Finals, the Boston Celtics beat the Los Angeles Lakers all seven times. Boston made it eight in 1984 in a classic series between the league's two biggest rivals.

- Behind superstar Michael Jordan, the Bulls won their sixth championship in eight years in 1998. To do so they defeated the Utah Jazz for the second straight year. The Jazz were led by the duo of Karl Malone and John Stockton.

- In 2013, the Miami Heat's star-studded lineup outlasted the San Antonio Spurs in seven games. The Heat were saved by a dramatic last-second shot in Game 6.

- By 2016, the city of Cleveland, Ohio, had not seen a major professional sports title in fifty-two years. Led by Ohio native LeBron James, the Cavaliers beat a historically successful Golden State Warriors team to end Cleveland's losing streak.

INTRODUCTION

WHERE LEGENDS ARE MADE

The final seconds in Game 7 of the 2016 NBA Finals were ticking down. The Cleveland Cavaliers led the Golden State Warriors 92–89. Cleveland's LeBron James took the pass from teammate Kyrie Irving in stride. James had a head of steam coming down the **lane**. He rose for a powerful dunk. As he brought his arm down, Golden State's Draymond Green fouled James hard.

James stayed down for a moment. But he rose to carry his team, and city,

LeBron James (right) collides with Draymond Green during Game 7 of the 2016 NBA Finals.

once again. After missing the first free throw, James hit the second. With a four-point lead and 10 seconds left, the victory was all but sealed. So was James's legacy as a hero in Cleveland.

THE BIGGEST STAGE

The NBA has long featured some of the most electrifying athletes on the planet. Many, like James, become legends for their performances in the NBA Finals. Each June, basketball fans tune in to see what kind of magic the best basketball players in the world will offer up next.

James backs into defender Klay Thompson during the 2016 NBA Finals.

1

CLASH OF THE TITANS

The Boston Celtics and the Los Angeles Lakers play on opposite sides of the country. Even so, the two teams have a heated basketball rivalry. It goes back to the early years of the league. The Celtics and Lakers always seemed to meet in the NBA Finals during the 1950s and 1960s.

However, in seven meetings, Boston won them all.

The teams met again in the 1984 Finals. Each team rolled in with a

Kevin McHale (left) of the Boston Celtics battles for a rebound with James Worthy (right) of the Los Angeles Lakers.

star-studded lineup. Boston was led by the fearsome front court of Kevin McHale, Robert Parish, and smooth-shooting Larry Bird.

The Lakers' **fast-breaking** offense was called "Showtime." Kareem Abdul-Jabbar, Michael Cooper, and James Worthy

BIRD VS. MAGIC

Fans had wanted to see Larry Bird and Magic Johnson match up in the NBA Finals since they were rookies in 1979. Earlier that year, Johnson's Michigan State University beat Bird's Indiana State University for the college championship. By 1984, Johnson had won two NBA championships. Bird had won one.

provided the dunks. Point guard Earvin "Magic" Johnson fed them the ball.

   The Lakers were in full flight during Game 1 in Boston, Massachusetts. Abdul-Jabbar's 32 points led the way in a 115–109 victory. Johnson had 10 **assists** as Los Angeles cruised.

   Game 2 came down to the wire. With 18 seconds left, the Lakers led 113–111. They were inbounding from their own end. After the pass in, Worthy tried to throw the ball across the court. Boston's Gerald Henderson intercepted it and scored a layup to tie the game.

The Lakers still had a chance to win on the last possession. But with Johnson dribbling, the time ran out without a Los Angeles shot. The Celtics took advantage of the mistakes to win 124–121 in overtime.

A HARD FOUL

Even with the loss, the Lakers could feel good heading back to Los Angeles, California. They only needed to win their three home games to take the series. They crushed Boston again in Game 3. Los Angeles's fast-break parade ended in a 137–104 **rout**.

Magic Johnson (center) led the NBA with an average of 13.1 assists per game in 1983–84.

The loss angered the ultra competitive Bird. He told reporters that his team had played soft in Game 3. His teammates got the message.

McHale wasn't usually a physical player. But with Boston trailing in the third quarter of Game 4, he hammered Los Angeles forward Kurt Rambis on a layup attempt. Rambis hit the floor hard, then popped up looking for a fight. McHale's play woke the Celtics up.

Boston rallied to force overtime. Then the Lakers crumbled. The Celtics went on to win 129–125. Late in the game, Johnson had made a few mistakes. As the series moved back to Boston, Celtics fans came up with a new nickname for the Lakers' star—"Tragic Johnson."

Larry Bird (33) averaged 27.4 points and 14.0 rebounds per game in the 1984 Finals.

TURNING UP THE HEAT

Johnson and the Lakers had to endure those taunts from Boston fans before Game 5. But the biggest problem during the game was the heat. Boston Garden had no air-conditioning. And the hot June day outside brought the temperature to 97°F (36°C) inside the arena. Referee Hugh Evans had to be replaced after suffering dehydration. Abdul-Jabbar needed an oxygen mask on the bench.

The only player who didn't seem to mind was Bird. He finished with game highs of 34 points and 17 rebounds. The Celtics won the "Heat Game" easily, 121–103. Now Boston was one win away from the title.

Back in Los Angeles for Game 6, the Celtics took a 65–59 lead into halftime. They still led by 4 after three quarters. Then Abdul-Jabbar and Johnson rose up.

Kareem Abdul-Jabbar (left) drives against Boston's Robert Parish.

Each player finished the game with a **double-double**. Los Angeles outscored Boston 36–21 in the final twelve minutes to win 119–108.

Game 7 was two nights later in Boston. By now both teams were battered and bruised. Before the game, Boston coach K.C. Jones told his team, "You're the best players in the world. Go out and prove it."[1]

The Celtics led by 14 in the fourth quarter. But with one minute to go the Lakers had cut that lead to three.

Los Angeles also had the ball in Johnson's hands. As Johnson went up for a jumper, Parish knocked the ball away. The Celtics hung on to win 111–102. The Lakers and Celtics played for the title again in 1985 and 1987. Los Angeles won them both.

Bird goes up for a shot in Game 7.

The rivalry between the two teams became a huge selling point for the NBA. It helped the league start growing into one of the most popular in the world.

2
ONE LAST SHOT

The Chicago Bulls ruled the NBA in the 1990s. They had two of the league's best players in guard Michael Jordan and forward Scottie Pippen. That duo led Chicago to three straight titles from 1991 to 1993. Chicago started a new streak in 1996. That year, the Bulls took home another title. In 1997, they topped the Utah Jazz in six games. One year later, the Bulls were back in the NBA Finals. Only the Jazz stood in the way of another Chicago "three-peat."

Michael Jordan (left) won his fifth career NBA Most Valuable Player (MVP) Award in 1997–98.

Pippen was great on offense and defense. Power forward Dennis Rodman was the game's best rebounder. But it was Jordan who ran the show. The megastar was by far the sport's best player in the 1990s.

Utah had its own high-powered pair, though. Point guard John Stockton and power forward Karl Malone were one of the best duos in the league. The Finals was set to be a series filled with **veterans**. All of those stars were over thirty.

Many thought the Jazz could win. The series had been close the year before.

Scottie Pippen goes up for a shot in Game 3 of the 1998 NBA Finals.

The Bulls were also nearing the end of their great run. Jordan was likely to retire after the season. Legendary coach Phil Jackson was not going to return. As the Finals opened, many wondered if Chicago could go out on top.

"It's a great feeling being the underdog because you want to go out now and prove everybody wrong," Pippen said before Game 1 started in Salt Lake City, Utah.[2]

CATCHING FIRE

Stockton scored 7 key points in overtime as the Jazz won Game 1 88–85. Jordan then scored 13 points in the fourth quarter as Chicago won Game 2 93–88. That put the Bulls in a good spot. The next three games were in Chicago, Illinois. The Bulls could wrap up the championship on their home floor with a sweep.

Game 3 was barely a contest. The Bulls led 17–14 after one quarter. From there, they took off. The Bulls entered the fourth

RECORD SETTER

Chicago's Game 3 rout set two NBA Finals records. The 42-point win was the largest in Finals history. The Jazz also scored the fewest points ever in an NBA Finals game.

quarter up 72–45. Jordan didn't even play in the fourth. Chicago won 96–54.

THE MAILMAN DELIVERS

Jordan had been the leading scorer in each of the first three games. He did it again in Game 4. But this time the Bulls needed all his 34 points. Jordan had 11 in the fourth quarter to hold off the Jazz's comeback attempt. Chicago won 86–82.

The Bulls had mostly shut down Stockton and Malone in the series. But Malone muscled his way through Game 5. The "Mailman" scored 25 of his

Karl Malone averaged 25.0 points and 10.5 rebounds per game in the 1998 Finals.

game-high 39 points in the second half. The Jazz won 83–81 to keep the series going.

Both Malone and Jordan were excellent in Game 6. In front of a rowdy crowd, the two superstars went back and forth.

At halftime, Jordan had 23 points. Malone had 20. The Jazz led 49–45.

A GOOD LOOK

Pippen had been having an excellent series. But a nagging back injury flared up in Game 6. As the game went on, it stiffened up. He barely played in the first half. He came back out for the second, but he wasn't very useful.

That meant Jordan had to shoulder the scoring load. But few players in NBA history were better under pressure. With 59 seconds left, Jordan sank two

Malone and Dennis Rodman (right) battle for a rebound.

free throws. He now had 41 points. And the game was tied 83–83.

On the next possession, Stockton hit a three-pointer to give Utah the lead. A Jordan layup then made it 86–85 Chicago.

On the next play, the Jazz threw the ball to Malone down low. Jordan raced in behind the big man and stole the ball with 18 seconds left.

All series long, the Jazz had used young guard Bryon Russell to guard Jordan. Russell liked to play physical defense. He got close to Jordan as the Bulls' star dribbled on the left wing with 10 seconds left. Jordan then quickly cut to the middle. As Russell followed, Jordan stopped near the free-throw line. Russell slipped. Now open, Jordan calmly hit the shot. The Bulls had the lead. "Great look. And it went in,"

Jordan goes up for his game-winning shot in Game 6.

Jordan said later. "I saw the moment. And I took advantage of the moment."[3]

The Bulls lead held when the Jazz missed a last-second shot. Jordan never played for Chicago again. His final act for the team was a game-winning shot for the team's sixth championship in eight years.

3

THE BIG THREE

Before the 2010–11 NBA season, the Miami Heat put together one of the flashiest lineups in league history. Miami had won an NBA title in 2006. That team was led by superstar shooting guard Dwyane Wade. In the summer of 2010, general manager Pat Riley brought in two more big names. All-star power forward Chris Bosh joined from the Toronto Raptors.

However, the biggest splash was bringing in LeBron James. The small forward was considered the best talent of his generation. "King James" left his hometown Cleveland Cavaliers to come to Miami and win a title.

Teaming LeBron James (6) and Chris Bosh (1) with Dwyane Wade (3) gave the Miami Heat three of the NBA's top players.

The so-called super team won its first championship in 2011–12. The Heat were back the next year to face the San Antonio Spurs. San Antonio also had a great collection of talent. The Spurs had won four titles since 1998–99. All four had featured steady superstar center Tim Duncan. Guards Manu Ginobili and Tony Parker were also veteran Spurs.

LOADED LINEUPS

The 2013 NBA Finals featured four players who had already won a Finals MVP Award. Tim Duncan had won it three times. Spurs guard Tony Parker won the award in 2007. Dwyane Wade was the 2006 MVP. And LeBron James had been the Finals MVP in 2012.

TRADING SHOTS

Game 1 in Miami, Florida, was one of the tightest in the series. James finished with a **triple-double**. But it wasn't enough, as the Spurs held Bosh and Wade in check. The Spurs rallied in the fourth quarter to win 92–88. Parker's bank shot with 5.2 seconds left sealed the victory.

    The Heat bounced back in a big way in Game 2. Once again Bosh and Wade were disappointing. The pair combined for only 22 points. But point guard Mario Chalmers stepped up to lead the team with 19. Miami routed the Spurs 103–84.

The series then moved to San Antonio, Texas. This time it was San Antonio's turn to run up the score. The Spurs hit a Finals-record 16 three-pointers in a 113–77 hammering.

James had been leading the Heat. Wade and Bosh finally got going in Game 4. The trio combined for 85 points in a 109–93 victory.

San Antonio coach Gregg Popovich made a lineup change before Game 5. All season long, Ginobili had come off the bench. Popovich moved him to the starting lineup. Ginobili made the move

The Spurs' Tony Parker (9) goes up for his game-clinching shot in the fourth quarter of Game 1.

pay off. He played his best game of the series. Ginobili scored 24 points and added 10 assists. The Spurs won 114–104.

Manu Ginobili reacts after hitting a shot in Game 5.

FROM THE CORNER

San Antonio needed one more win as the teams shifted back to Miami. The Spurs took a 10-point lead into the fourth quarter of Game 6. Duncan had already piled up

30 points. But the Heat held him scoreless the rest of the way. And Miami started to claw back.

The Spurs still led 94–89 with 28.2 seconds left. James missed a three-pointer, but Heat forward Mike Miller grabbed the offensive rebound. Miller passed it back to James, who drilled his second chance to make it 94–92.

The Heat still needed to extend the game. Miller did that by fouling San Antonio's Kawhi Leonard. The Spurs forward sank only one of two free throws, leaving the score 95–92.

James was once again the top option at the other end. But he missed his shot. Both teams battled for the rebound. This time Bosh grabbed the board. As he did, veteran guard Ray Allen backed behind the three-point line in the corner.

Allen was one of the best three-point shooters in league history. He had been a star player earlier in his career. Now thirty-seven, he had joined the Heat as a backup.

Bosh tossed the ball to Allen just as the guard set his feet. As Parker closed in, Allen rose and hit the game-tying shot.

Miami fans celebrate behind Ray Allen after his game-tying three-point shot in Game 6.

The crowd in Miami's American Airlines Center erupted. For the moment, the season was saved.

43

Miami won 103–100 in overtime. The talk of the night was Allen's legendary shot. Few of his teammates were surprised it went in. "If there's one guy you want to have the ball in that situation, it's Walter Ray Allen," said Heat forward Shane Battier.[4]

THE KING IS CROWNED

Allen's clutch shot had overshadowed James's huge game. James finished Game 6 with 32 points, 10 rebounds, and 11 assists.

James jumped right back into the spotlight for Game 7. He played all but

James (left) holds up the NBA Finals MVP Award as he celebrates with teammate Dwyane Wade after the Heat's victory in Game 7.

three minutes. James's 37 points were the most in a Game 7 since 1969. With the 95–88 win, the Heat were champions for the second straight year.

4
BRINGING IT HOME

Entering the 2015–16 NBA season, the city of Cleveland, Ohio, was hungry for a major sports title. The city had not seen a championship since football's Browns had won it all in 1964. Many thought that would change when the Cavaliers drafted Akron, Ohio, native LeBron James in 2003.

The young superstar brought the Cavs to the Finals in 2007, but they lost.

In 2010, James left the team to sign with the Miami Heat. After winning two titles there, he returned to Cleveland in 2014–15.

LeBron James puts in a layup during the 2016 NBA Finals.

And he promised the city he would bring home a championship.

It wasn't going to be easy. In 2015, the Cavaliers lost the Finals to the Golden State Warriors. The next season, the Warriors won an NBA-record seventy-three games. Coach Steve Kerr's team was loaded with talent. Guards Steph Curry and Klay Thompson were known as the "Splash Brothers" for their great shooting. Forward Draymond Green was a force inside. The 2016 Finals was set to be an epic rematch.

Despite a near triple-double from James, the Warriors raced out to a 104–89 win

Golden State's Draymond Green goes up for a shot in Game 2

in Game 1. Game 2 was even more of a wipeout. Led by Green's 28 points, the Warriors smashed Cleveland 110–77.

James and guard Kyrie Irving each topped 30 points in Game 3. Playing at home, Cleveland bounced back with a 120–90 win. But the series looked over after Golden State's 108–97 win in Game 4. Even worse for Cleveland, the series was headed back to Oakland, California. The Warriors had lost only three home games all season.

THE COMEBACK

James was a do-it-all 6-foot-9 forward. He had nearly posted triple-doubles in all three losses. But he needed help if the Cavaliers were going to hold up his promise to the city of Cleveland. Some of the Cavaliers' other big stars needed to step up.

That help arrived from Irving in Game 5. The guard erupted for 41 points. He shot 17-for-24 from the field. James matched Irving with 41 points of his own. He also had 16 rebounds and seven assists. Cleveland won 112–97 to stay alive.

The teams went back in Cleveland for Game 6. The Cavaliers raced out to a 59–43 halftime lead behind 20 points

SUSPENSION

The Cavaliers received a boost in Game 5 from the suspension of Warriors star Draymond Green. The feisty forward had been ejected late in Game 4 for hitting LeBron James.

from Irving. James took over in the second half. He finished with 41 points again, along with eight rebounds, eleven assists, four **steals**, and three blocks. Cleveland won 115–101 to force Game 7.

THE BLOCK

The teams were met by a roaring crowd at Oakland's Oracle Arena. Roughly 31 million fans were watching on television. They tuned in to a duel between James and Green in the first half. James led Cleveland with 12 points. But Green had 22, and the Warriors took a 7-point halftime lead.

MOST NBA FINALS MVP AWARDS*

- **Michael Jordan** 6 (1991, 1992, 1993, 1996, 1997, 1998)
- **LeBron James** 4 (2012, 2013, 2016, 2020)
- **Magic Johnson** 3 (1980, 1982, 1987)
- **Shaquille O'Neal** 3 (2000, 2001, 2002)
- **Tim Duncan** 3 (1999, 2003, 2005)

*Through the 2021–22 season

Source: "NBA History—Finals MVP," ESPN, n.d. www.espn.com.

Only Michael Jordan has won the NBA Finals MVP Award more times than LeBron James.

James struggled to shoot in the third quarter. He made up for it by dishing out five assists. Irving had 12 of the Cavaliers' 33 points in the quarter. As the fourth quarter opened, Cleveland trailed by only one point.

James's shooting came back in the fourth. He scored 11 of Cleveland's 18 points. But his biggest play came on defense.

The teams were tied 89–89 with two minutes left. Irving drove to the basket and missed. As both teams scrambled for the rebound, four Cavaliers ended up under the offensive basket. There was only one man back to stop Golden State forward Andre Iguodala as he dribbled up court.

Iguodala thought he had an easy layup to take the lead. But James sprinted the length of the floor. Just as Iguodala put the ball up

James's thunderous block on Andre Iguodala late in Game 7 turned the momentum back to Cleveland's side.

on the backboard, a flying James swatted the shot. "The Block" had saved the day.

The Cavaliers still needed to score. Neither team had scored for nearly four minutes. Irving finally hit a three-pointer over Curry with 53 seconds left.

The Warriors had the best three-point shooter in league history on the roster in Curry. But on the next possession, he missed a game-tying shot. James then sealed the 93–89 win with a free throw. The Cavaliers had kept the high-powered Warriors from scoring for the final 4:39 of the game.

"I'm coming home with what I said I was going to do," James said after the game. "I can't wait to get off that plane, hold that trophy up and see all our fans."[5]

Cleveland fans hold up signs thanking the team after the Cavaliers' win in Game 7.

Cleveland became the first team to ever win the Finals after trailing 3–1. Three days after Game 7, a huge crowd turned out for Cleveland's victory parade. They saved the biggest cheers for James.

GLOSSARY

assists

passes that result in made baskets

double-double

an accumulation of at least ten in two different statistical categories in a game, such as points and rebounds

fast-breaking

moving the ball up the court quickly in order to score easy baskets

lane

the area near the basket that runs from the baseline to the free-throw line

rout

a victory by a lopsided margin

steals

plays that take the ball away from a player on the other team

triple-double

an accumulation of at least ten in three different statistical categories in a game, such as points, rebounds, and assists

veterans

players who have been professionals for several seasons

SOURCE NOTES

CHAPTER ONE: CLASH OF THE TITANS

1. Quoted in "Legends from Celtics & Lakers Share Favorite Memories of Storied Rivalry," *WBZ-CBS News Boston*, January 30, 2021. www.cbsnews.com.

CHAPTER TWO: ONE LAST SHOT

2. Quoted in Terry Armour, "Chicago Bulls Head into the 1998 NBA Finals Against the Utah Jazz as Underdogs: 'You Want to Go Out Now and Prove Everybody Wrong,'" *Chicago Tribune,* June 3, 1998. www.chicagotribune.com.

3. Quoted in Mike Wise, "THE N.B.A. FINALS; A Steal, a Shot and One More Crown," *New York Times*, June 15, 1998. www.nytimes.com.

CHAPTER 3: THE BIG THREE

4. Quoted in Harvey Araton, "Heat's Allen Knows All About Hitting Big 3-Pointers," *New York Times*, June 19, 2013. www.nytimes.com.

CHAPTER 4: BRINGING IT HOME

5. Quoted in "Cavaliers Become First Team to Rally from 3–1 Series Deficit in NBA Finals," *Associated Press*, June 20, 2016. www.espn.com.

FOR FURTHER RESEARCH

BOOKS

Alexander Lowe, *G.O.A.T. Basketball Power Forwards*. Minneapolis, MN: Lerner Publications, 2023.

Brian Mahoney, *GOATs of Basketball*. Minneapolis, MN: Abdo Publishing, 2022.

David Stabler, *Inside the Golden State Warriors*. Minneapolis, MN: Lerner Publications, 2023.

INTERNET SOURCES

Anthony Cotton, "Green and White and Red All Over," *Sports Illustrated*, June 25, 1984. www.vault.si.com.

John Jefferson Tan, "'All It Took Was One Touch on That Black Line, and It's a Different Story'—Ray Allen on His Thrilling Game 6 Dagger Against the Spurs," *Basketball Network*, February 28, 2023. www.basketballnetwork.net.

Ian Thompson, "In America: The End of a Stellar NBA Generation," *New York Times*, June 6, 1998. www.nytimes.com.

WEBSITES

Basketball Reference
www.basketball-reference.com

Basketball Reference is a research website that offers accurate statistical data for every game and player ever associated with the NBA.

Naismith Memorial Basketball Hall of Fame
www.hoophall.com

Hoophall.com is the official site of the Naismith Memorial Basketball Hall of Fame, located in Springfield, Massachusetts. This website features information on the museum's exhibits and events as well as enshrined members and basketball history.

National Basketball Association
www.nba.com

NBA.com is the official website of the National Basketball Association and all thirty of its franchises.

INDEX

Abdul-Jabbar, Kareem, 12–13, 18
Allen, Ray, 42, 44

Battier, Shane, 44
Bird, Larry, 12, 15, 18
Bosh, Chris, 35, 37–38, 42

Chalmers, Mario, 37
Cooper, Michael, 12
Curry, Steph, 48, 56

Duncan, Tim, 36, 40, 53

Ginobili, Manu, 36, 38–39
Green, Draymond, 7, 48–49, 51, 52

Henderson, Gerald, 13

Iguodala, Andre, 54
Irving, Kyrie, 6, 49, 51–54, 56

Jackson, Phil, 26
James, LeBron, 6–8, 35, 36, 37–38, 41–42, 44–45, 46–57
Johnson, Magic, 12, 13–14, 16–18, 20, 53
Jones, K.C., 20
Jordan, Michael, 22, 24, 26, 28–33, 53

Kerr, Steve, 48

Leonard, Kawhi, 41

Malone, Karl, 24, 28–30, 32
McHale, Kevin, 12, 16
Miller, Mike, 41

Parish, Robert, 12, 20
Parker, Tony, 36–37, 42
Pippen, Scottie, 22, 24, 26, 30
Popovich, Gregg, 38

Rambis, Kurt, 16
Riley, Pat, 34
Rodman, Dennis, 24
Russell, Bryon, 32

Stockton, John, 24, 26, 28, 31

Thompson, Klay, 48

Wade, Dwyane, 34, 36–38
Worthy, James, 12–13

IMAGE CREDITS

Cover: © Marcio Jose Sanchez/AP Images
5: © Lev Radin/Shutterstock Images
7: © Michael Macor/San Francisco Chronicle/AP Images
9: © Marcio Jose Sanchez/AP Images
11: © Peter Southwick/AP Images
15: © John W. McDonough/Icon Sportswire/AP Images
17: © Focus on Sport/Getty Images Sport/Getty Images
19: © Elise Amendola/AP Images
21: © Kevin Reece/Icon Sportswire/AP Images
23: © Mark J. Terrill/AP Images
25: © Fred Jewell/AP Images
29: © Mark J. Terrill/AP Images
31: © Mark J. Terrill/AP Images
33: © Chuck Wing/Deseret News/AP Images
35: © Lynne Sladky/AP Images
39: © Wilfredo Lee/AP Images
40: © Eric Gay/AP Images
43: © Lynne Sladky/AP Images
45: © Lynne Sladky/AP Images
47: © Carlos Avila Gonzalez/San Francisco Chronicle/AP Images
49: © Marcio Jose Sanchez/AP Images
53: © Red Line Editorial
55: © Eric Risberg/AP Images
57: © Eric Risberg/AP Images

ABOUT THE AUTHOR

Ethan Olson is a sportswriter and editor based in Minneapolis, Minnesota.